A JUMP START

A JUMP START

JAMES LASDUN

W · W · NORTON & COMPANY
New York   London

ISBN 0-393-02582-9

W. W. Norton & Company, Inc., 500 Fifth Avenue,
New York, N. Y. 10110
W. W. Norton & Company Ltd., 37 Great Russell Street,
London WC1B 3NU
1 2 3 4 5 6 7 8 9 0

FOR PIA

CONTENTS

ACKNOWLEDGEMENTS

Acknowledgements are due to the following:

Encounter, Fiction Magazine, Firebird 3 (Penguin Books), *The Gregory Awards Anthology 1981 & 1982* (Carcanet), *Literary Review, National Poetry Competition Anthology, Paris Review, Poetry Book Society Christmas Supplement 1986, Twofold, Waves, West Africa, Boulevard, Paris Review, Pequod*

'On the Road to Chenonceaux' was first published in a limited edition by Giles and Jonathan Leaman.

A JUMP START

Fate, in a painter's shape, began to dip
His brush in wet vermilion, letting drip
Every minute or so one beady gout
Onto the street below . . .

                      Meanwhile a shout
Of triumph told me that the job was done –
Each wished-for detail gathered into one
Wrapped-round expanse of yellow silk, held tight
About her waist – a fluted fall of light,
Half-light and shadow, billowing at the sleeves –
Picture a ship's bell melting, harvest sheaves,
Their brilliance hatching with the crack of dawn,
Gold cobbled light on streams – I could go on,
But what I most remember is the way
She wore it; buckled turbulence, the spray
Of water on zinc, a beehive's boiling throng,
The way a budded peony breasts the strong
Rotunda of its sheath; improbable
Compression, not of flesh, but of the soul,
As if she'd torn through every veil, but found
Matter itself in Purdah, nature bound
And yashmak'd in some chemical Sharia
She'd never overthrow. Her heart's desire
Rippled in the mirror, and she turned
Quickly; the knowledge framed inside it burned
Too violently . . .

                She wore it from the shop
And step by step we zeroed on the drop –
Slick globule that prefigured my one spurt
Of infidelity (I blabbed, the hurt
Exploded in her body like a gun)
Oh Exegetes, behold her now, the sun
Falling upon her in gambades and curls
Of gold, the whipped-cream, thixotropic swirls
Of virgin silk notating on the air
The way a body registers despair;

I see it in slow motion: the surprise,
The torso's whiplash twist, neck arched, the eyes
Widening as the tugged silk slides around,
And with it, like a perfect bullet wound,
One molten ruby. Silence. *No harm done;*
Nothing we can't put right (much later on
The same words met the same astonished look);
Endings are swift – we taxied home, she took
The dress off, checked the damage, nodded, gripped
A bunch of fabric in each fist, and ripped.

D. C.

Co-Pilot: Larry, we're going down Larry.
Pilot: I know it.

Chill-seeded mildew, winter crystals,
        America, raddled rose –
New Year's Eve, the gin runs over the sloes
        Slick, sluggish as the trickles
        Of the ice-locked Potomac.

We packed a killer whale in crushed ice
        To fly it from the Maine coast
Down to Marine City, declares a guest
        (Sweet pixilated features,
        Diamonds all over her breast

Clattering like impacted blossom) –
        A small crowd gathers around;
She talks insouciantly, ungloves a hand
        And freezes: slippery varnish
        Has streaked her fingers crimson

Like a butcher's. Midnight. Someone sings
        We'll drink a cup of kindness –
Outside, the ice is lacquering the wings
        Of aircraft on the runways;
        A crystal integument

Thick enough to bring them crashing down
        Like bloated, over-ripe fruit –
Elsewhere a visitor slews into town
        Rigid in his cold mantle,
        His mouth full of splintered ice.

6

A day painted like a child's room
In bright colours; red pillar box
Where Loomis mailed your pristine letters
(Deferential among his betters
He tipped his hat to us), pink bloom
Of blossom ruched like dancers' frocks –

We passed a constable in blue
Guarding your door against – what?
Avenging citizens who'd voted
For someone else? Your own much-quoted
'Essential labour surplus' who
Would give their pittance to see you shot?

Your house revealed a curious taste
For hybrid forms; a figurine
Fused into a branch of coral
Was Daphne changing to a laurel,
And in a mounted shell were placed
Glass lilies, stained frost-white and green –

A cultivated passion, yet
Quite in keeping with your own
Change from dignified Patrician
To our 'Most Pelted Politician'
Glistening absurdly with the wet
Pearl and gold of an eggshell crown;

And what would you say if you knew
That I was among the enemy?
I, who had eaten at your table,
Barracking, though still unable
To hurl more than abuse at you,
Keeping my head down guiltily –

How would you accommodate
Such treachery, could you admire
One who'd sacrifice his class's
Better interest to the mass's,
Or would you tell me what I hate
Is what I secretly desire?

A JUMP START

Daybreak, already dangerous, trapped
By her own tactics in a pencil-skirt
And high-heels for an interview (M. Phil
    In Women's Studies), out she stepped
        Onto the slippery path,
        Gripping my arm so tight it hurt,
Puffing a white ellipsis onto the chill –

The car was in a slick of mud;
You'd better lift me . . . Overhead an oak
Sighed, and released a dead leaf from its limbs –
    Down it fluttered as the battery died,
        A dream of impotence –
        She leaned across me, yanked the choke,
But I couldn't raise a spark, then up he swims,

Up he floats out of the dark, his face
Lapping the window till I rolled it down,
My solitary country neighbour – *sounds as if*
    (The words fish-bubbling out, his voice
        Fathoms deep in whisky)
    Your battery's dead . . . I felt the frown
Massing beside me as she watched her life

Stretch out thin as a gossamer strand
Held perilously intact by nothing more
Than a drunkard's whim of kindness – off he went
    For jump-leads – I could see her mind,
        A Sisyphus shouldering
        Time itself (I'd seen that look before;
A vow to give up smoking, bafflement

9

At the sheer nothingness, as if
There should have been a shoal of butts to smoke
Backwards to a healed and pristine white . . .)
We heard his flat tyres crunch the drive –
Time's wingless chariot –
Silenus on a wineskin, soak
Vined in his tangled leads – he couldn't quite

Remember what they were – she called
Instructions from the car. I stood outside,
A bandsman beating two-time with one hand,
Triple-time out of the other, pulled
Between her tight-packed rage
And his slubbery fumbling, as we tried,
The two of us, two men, to make a stand

In this last corner of our realm;
Machinery . . . The final moment clears
From a blur of clips to a burst of high
Cold laughter as I brushed his arm
And we leaped up in shock,
A million brilliant snowdrop spears
Flashing like mica schist at the whitening sky.

The colour of a not quite bloodless coup –
Madeira, tawny port, the rusty hulls
Of tankers on the Tagus . . . Mineral-rich,
Premonitory, a shade
That stalked us through the country
From the first morning when we stood
Over the Alfama's terracotta tiles
Watching the caged canaries flap
Like apprehension in our heads
Until it faded, and these almost-reds
Welled up, and bled into the gap;

Colour of our necessary silences,
Of infidelities suspected, known,
Of unforgiven spite, loveless embraces,
Our cosmic mismatch: Taurus/Gemini –
Your bullish pride, my two or more faces . . .
We steer between these rocks and pools,
Past mansions like rococo chests of drawers,
Their balconies pulled open, spilling out
Veils and tresses of blue starry flowers,
Through Sintra where a lush mist drools
Over Beckford's garden exile, Monserrate –

Palm trees among the evergreens, lilyponds,
Sweetpeas and crozier ferns – transported here,
Sun-fed, drenched, we're like a big-leafed plant
Returned to its ancestral soil
And finding for the first time unexpected
Brilliant blooms among its stalks and fronds –
Your camera finger twitches, and you coil
Quintas, abbeys, mountains, onto film,

Ceaselessly, as if you meant
To outmanoeuvre fate with resurrected
Opulence, glazed thin as sacrament,
When this becomes as if it never was –

I watch you dozing on a hotel bed,
Your body brimming in a swimsuit clasp,
Breath swells your flesh against it, risen bread,
Voluptuary, your one-piece rucked
Up at your groin, a creamy littoral
Beaching the sunburn on your thighs and hips –
My Pasiphaë . . . the sex-smile at your lips
Confides a dream like hers, of being fucked
By silky haunches strutting on the cusp
Of bestial and divine – Poseidon's bull,
Surf-white and rippling like atlantic swell . . .

A myth for the jilted – that nothing human
Can take their place . . . and how the myth consoles
When fields of cork trees flayed to coppery boles,
Goldfish in murky water, or the tanned
Saddlery of hams slung from a beam
Shimmer in recollection like a dream
Of falling; so the present bleeds
Back into the past, and a lover
Willing a silent telephone to ring
Becomes the unarmed toreador we saw
Taunting a stubborn bull the goads had left
Unweakened, till suddenly it charged
And rammed him straight against the pen
Six feet below us in the furrowed sand,
His toppled body crushed, and bright with gore,
The bull led out alive to fight again.

SNAKE BURNING

Indolent creature, do you not observe
How the air is clotting with locusts? Coil
Upon coil of you wreathes the dead acacia –
Such heavy lumber to shift, such toil
To unravel yourself, each loop and curve –

I know that tired complexity, I too
Would choose to think this heat the sun's alone –
Your tongue is mine, and we both taste burning
But lie as if our minds had turned to stone.
We could outsleep the limbs that cradle you.

Look now, the earth about you is alive:
Plum-sized shrews, the golden field mice,
And spark-bright lizards scuttle past your jaws.
A hare stumbles against you, mazed butterflies
Gyrate. The air is humming like a hive,

Ground trembling beneath you, while overhead
In swift succession, deer and gazelle leap,
Trailing their shadows across your body –
Wisps of blue smoke arrive, and still you sleep;
What is it you and I cannot feel? Dread –

Until the fury is upon us: fire
Blazing in the grass, do you feel it now?
Pooled in your contortions, furnacing –
You flex and writhe, but you have become slow
And each nerve seems to sing like a plucked wire –

I watch you dying; are we so alike
Our deaths could be exchanged? I am entranced –
Your last prey – watching your glazed marquetry
Scorch, your body dance as it always danced,
Your diamond head thrown back as if to strike.

CRABS

— whose flesh retracted from a violent shore
To lie beneath a carapace of bone,
Who lost the end of living in the means,
Each in its private military zone,

Paradigms of the exoskeletal,
Whose armature and claws' serrated grip
Taught us technologies of the metal muscle,
Gave us machines to scavenge, crack or rip —

We netted crabs out from Menemsha Pond
Risking our naked flesh against the bite
Of bladed oyster shells and hidden claws,
Crashing the gaudy creatures into light

Where, with their turquoise streaks and bevelled limbs,
They seemed some dormant possibility
The mind had once considered as a shell
Against the issue of its own proclivity

To violence. They battled in the keep tank,
And later, when we pulled them out, we saw
They'd necklaced like a conjuror's magic hoops,
Leaving behind one frayed and severed claw.

Dolphins at every corner, bees
The size of fists, and pinecones
Bigger than the Pope's crown –
    But all of these,
Like the million frilled scallop shells
    Cropping up as fonts or
    Merely gratuitous scagliola,
    Were of granite, basalt, porphyry:

The organic lapsed into stone,
    A city yearning to be wilderness
Again – but not really;
    Keeping these mascots
Like photos of an ex who might occasionally
    Lubricate a fantasy
    But whose bodily presence
    Would only embarrass.

I was near the Quirinale barracks,
    Outside a walled garden (foamy
    Overspill of jasmine and white lilac)
        When I saw it –
Stockstill on the pavement, shocked rigid
    By its drop from Paradise,
    Head like a little flint arrow
    Cocked up in astonishment,

Body a nothing, a brittle twig,
    A thin bean-pod into which
    Some whimsical garden-god had squirted
        A volt of life –
An afterthought, a scribble; pencilled into creation,
    As easily erased;
    I nudged it lightly, expecting
    An electric, trigger-reflex scuttle

To safety – but it hardly moved,
Then wouldn't move at all, except to slide
Where I pushed it (suction-pad feet
    Splayed out like tiny flowers)
But its weakness was like a fulcrum over which
My own strength seemed to pivot, as it stared
At its greenless future in an impossible
Mineral kingdom, and refused it.

ABOVE LAGGAN

Low sun, low mist, long shadows probe the water,
Wild cotton flares in the contracting dusk,
The harebells flex to voltage in the stalk
And wheatgerm stiffens in its husk –
Down on the fallow field the rabbits scatter
Maddened by the shadow of a hawk.

Whoever looks desires that proximate death;
To flare like matchlight, stiffen, flex or run,
Somehow to evade the supernumerary,
To have one's shadow lengthened by the sun
And hold, elect, one's tenantry of earth
Whereof all things are but a colonie –

You could lie here imagining chance might fall
From nowhere, like a hawk, or that the wind,
To whose calligraphy the hill-grass yields,
Might write as vividly across the mind,
Leaving indelible the kestrel's call,
Cloud-shadow spreading stains across the fields.

JUMPING

He meets you at the zoo. You stand and watch
The mossy, boulder-headed bison hump
Their buttressed tonnage round a patch of dust,
A cayman's eyelid flash its mineral sump,
Flamingos, sea-shell pink, curled up asleep
On cocktail stems of leg, a cheetah pick
The last pink shred of membrane from a bone,
Insect analogies of leaf and stick . . .
A brochure of solutions – every feature
Fashioned like serrations on a key
To prise existence from a precise world
As far from here as yours is. What you see
Mirrors in wing and tusk, night-eyes, webbed feet,
Your own precise and private arsenal
For getting by – each weapon obsolete.

So you permit him to walk you home,
Assenting as he hovers at the door,
As if assent were all you had to lock
What happens now with what has gone before –
This ice-thin plateau of the present, poised
Like crystal on a juggler's column –
Miracles of balance hold you here,
Tremulous, a stranger in your room
Eyeing the bed, the map pinned on the wall –
He makes a tease of searching for your town –
His fingers brush Alaska, skim the Yukon,
Rockies, *warmer warmer*, plunging down
Nebraska, Oklahoma, *further south*,
Tracing the Mississippi, *hot that's hot*,
Vicksburg, Louisiana, the hot mouth . . .

Then by and by your moon-lit bodies sprawl
Entangled. You're asleep but not at rest,
Flushed hot and cold, an ember's red-black shimmer,
Your face a frown, twitching on his breast –
Wherever you are you're not here;
That muscle quivering in your hip
Is fear of heights – you're balanced on a ledge,
And miles beneath you, willing you to slip,
Behemoth, Cockatrice, misshapen hybrid
Slavering in shadow; the day's nightmare
Spawn of beast on reptile, bird on fish –
And then you jump, and crashing through the air
Towards you comes the creature of your dream,
Its double head familiar . . . one is yours,
The other's watching as you wake, and scream.

THE JAGUAR'S DREAM

after Leconte de Lisle

Lianas in bright bloom hang from mahogany shade,
Motionless where the air is languorous
And buzzing with summer flies. Brushing the moss,
They curl into cradles clutched by the emerald quetzal, swayed
Wildly by monkeys, spun with the yellow spider's silver floss.
Here the bull-killer, slayer of stallions, tired,
Moves among dead tree-stumps moist and soft as sponge,
Implicit violence in his measured tread,
Pelt shimmering with each muscle's plunge,
While from his bay-wide muzzle, drooping with thirst,
A clipped, harsh, rattled breathing shocks
Huge lizards from their sun-trance to a burst
Of chrome-green sparkling over shadowed rocks;
And there where the dark wood blots the sun,
He sprawls across a lichened stone,
Licks satin paws to a lustrous sheen,
Flutters the sleep-heavy lids of gold eyes down
And, as the ghost of his waking force
Twitches his tail and ripples along each side,
He dreams that by some orchard's water course
He leaps and digs his dripping claws
Into a bellowing bull's flesh-swollen hide.

THE REFUGEES

a variation on 'Les Éléphants' by Leconte de Lisle

Stilled undulations of orange sand . . .
A boiled-dry ocean's crater left on the heat
To deliquesce, lay smouldering in that land
Of sleep and silence. Under the bearded palms

Lions lolled their desiccated tongues
In air like copper vapour . . . not a bird
To stir it; up on high a beaten gong's
Swollen aorta pulsed gold shimmering light –

'Vast the space inflamed burning under the clear skies'
But into this emptiness they come, the voyagers,
Slow compañeros, wrinkled, lumbering,
Visions of homeland blurred in their sand-scoured eyes,

Out front, his king-in-exile's Lydian trudge
Crumbling the dunes, a mountain-headed Moses
Compacts in haunches fissured like the bark
Of a bulged-out oak, the vast, corroding rage

Of dispossession – leading past the bleached
Carcasses of jeeps, an ivory cache
Of propped up mortar shells, a crashed
Wingless jet half-buried like a beached

Still-grinning whale (its hull so hot a touch
Would set a finger sizzling like a steak) . . .
Gross, swollen bellies, hunger-furrowed ribs,
Flesh blistered to bladderwrack, blackened scabs

Strafed to a turquoise smoulder by the flies –
Human, pachyderm, war's baleful hybrids,
Bemonstered hierophants of mysteries
Too bright for human eyes, they've tramped the id's

Slumlands for too long; now in their dreams
Of moonlit forests where moist orchids bloom
Brilliantly in shadow, or green hills
Draped in a braided tress of silver streams,

What comforts most? The thought of how they'll stand
Among crushed canes and rushes, drinking skies
Mirrored in crystal waters, or the thought
Of how they'll drive us out from Paradise?

HERMAPHRODITUS

after Ovid

The day hot, and the pool so clear
You could have counted every stone,
I thought I'd break my journey there –
I drank until I'd quenched my thirst,
Then thinking I was quite alone

Stripped off and bathed, first in the sun,
Letting the heat caress my skin
(Its weightless touch the only one
I'd ever known), then dipped a foot,
Lowered my body gently in –

And then I saw her on the bank,
'My name' she said 'Is Salmacis,
This pool is mine, each drop you drank
Will cost you – ' here she pursed her lips,
Half closed her eyes, and smiled, ' – a kiss.'

I blushed – the crystal water hid
Nothing from her shameless eyes,
She reached and pulled me to her side –
Ignorant of love's mysteries,
I let her press my lips to hers –

At first it tasted sweet and cool
But then I felt her grip my waist
As if she'd hoist me from the pool
And suck the last breath out of me,
And so desire's brief sweet taste

Turned to the sour taste of fear –
I struggled free and turned about
To cross the pool and run from her,
But where the shore had been, sheer cliffs
Now towered, leaving no way out –

She stood there laughing on the bank,
Uncoiled the garlands from her hair,
Loosened her tunic, while I shrank,
Trembling, to the cliff to see
The white silk lay her soft flesh bare;

A wind blew through the cypress trees,
The sun dropped down behind a hill,
I felt the shadowed water freeze
About my naked skin, while she
Raised up her arms, and laughing still,

Plunged in and twisted like an eel
Beneath the shimmering water: I
Could hardly move – she clutched my heel
And rising, wound her body round
My own, like ivy round a tree

Until she held me face to face,
My limbs in hers – I pushed, she clung,
And as I fought her tight embrace
The pool turned black as if the dregs
We'd stirred were of some noxious dung –

I felt my body going slack,
And hers (although you couldn't see
Whose limbs were whose inside that murk),
'Now Gods' she cried, 'let this sweet boy
Remain forever joined with me.'

The last word came from my own lips
And in the turbid water now
Upon my own, a woman's hips
Were swelling, and upon my breast
A woman's . . . So I came to know

How the cowardly in love
And the too-brave are the same fool;
I bear my double shape for proof,
And any lovers thus entwined
Bathe in Hermaphroditus's pool.

At best the sparkle on the chain of being;
At worst an itch,
A superfetation,
The seconds-younger twin of sex,
Resembling it as greed resembles hunger.

It was the cool of the evening,
The cruising hour;
Shoals of eyes quivered pair on pair,
Till a spark in the jelly blew the circuit –
You had to pitch yourself just above animal,

Just below human – a tight-rope
I wobbled on for three months;
Joe Allen's, The Closerie, Rose Bon-Bon,
Gobbling on eyes, oysters, oestrogen . . .
I was turning iridescent.

I came to my senses in a quayside bar –
An iris of purplish tiddlers round an ochre blob
Bobbing on the water, then a dish
Of the same but stiffened, lustrous fry
Set before me . . . I had to move –

It was one thing or the other –
Dead air crammed with sweetnesses –
Creams, effluvia streaming from the yachts,
Winking oil-froth, a swarm
Of sheeny girls on mopeds;

One of them landed ten yards from me;
I strolled up, a shambles of mime, and she
Was off like a bluebottle,
Publishing my disgrace
On a scroll of shimmering air . . .

VINDICE AT THE
OYSTER BAR

for Robin Robertson

Here they come, the silver-haired boys,
Minds glandular, tuned to the brine of sex,
Bullion at flinty wrists, carbuncled fingers,
Silk scarves afloat on scalloped necks –

You foolish girls, so willingly deceived,
What do you seek, to what ghost of bliss
Glimpsed beyond silver do you cling? Rose flesh
Turning to carrion for the next jackal's kiss . . .

A parable: watch light blade down through blinds
To tongue bright morning's tocsin from a jar
And coax a glass-hard tulip's metal scarlet,
The belling petals' aztec star –

One day you touch the flower, and each petal
Drops from the stem unblemished, hard, with all
Its moon-curve, pristine glaze immaculate,
You almost hear them clatter as they fall –

That is the unimpeachable life;
To quit before the years' contusions bloom,
Unheralded, each second like the spider's
Perilous march across a crowded room;

Then watch those crayfish in the bubbling tank,
Curled peach-fire torsos peppered like your wrist,
Splayed samurai tails, the stripped-flex feelers
Beckoning what the body must resist;

More intimacy than nature will allow –
Look at them grope, and probe, and interlace
Through drifts of snapped antennae, severed limbs,
Love fused to violence in the one embrace;

I see your backs thrash, limbs flail, as theirs do
When the bare-armed scullion wrenches one pair
Out from that slow, obscene, dissolution,
Into the quick, asphyxiating air.

VINDICE AT THE
OPENING NIGHT

The season's colour is white; champagne's
Clear crucible for cream sash,
Silk, pearls, a bitten shrimp, flesh white as ash
On men whose eye-whites, teeth, bright chains
Ignite in ultra-violet, flash-bulb flash –
Mushroom-light, endive, a salad of light
Tossed on the dance floor where we're driven
Blenched leaves in a dry storm's uneven
Gusts – and we're almost angels tonight,
Without a heaven: this is our heaven –

A halo dazzles in your blonde hair,
You trail me, bag in one hand,
Shoes in the other, a jetlag's brilliant
Hoar-frost lustre on cheeks as rare
As a pollution sunset, the gold band
At your wrist splintering to a fine gold down
Strewn across your arm . . . I feel you clutching
My hand as I retreat, and I'm wishing
Your diamonds' crushed millenia were my own,
My heart gone crystal in a camera's flashing –

ADDRESS TO VINDICE

Peace Vindice, the chiselled marble holds
Your love's impacted shards; nothing can touch
That singular, effaced complexion. The dead
Seldom betray the living; no humid
Masculine embrace can thaw that ice –
And look, she does not resurrect herself
After each mourning, brazenly alive,
Brazenly, treading the same streets as you,
Imminent at corners, a blank stare
Drowned in a carriage window as you halt
Adjacent in a tunnel till the moment's
Elision stretches outward, and as if
She'd *never* had the choice, she disappears.

Echoing in the galleries . . . or days
Dull as a lover's past – days when a song
You thought came out that year, was after all
A decade old – recall them now, the long
Hot afternoons, time sticky in its glaze

Of too much humid sky; days when you'd watch
The widow from the basement stand
Hours on end in the public phone
Chattering, while her eloquent hand
Bunched up, as if it didn't matter much

That the line was dead; Oh bright scintillae,
Photons, gravitons, the hidden shirr
Of substance; final, indivisible
Iotas that must move, or disappear –
Recessions of light that leave a human body

Thin as a shadow, spectral, feather-blown,
Spinning among the self's unlit cortège
Of ghost selves aching for the something lost
When mirrors leave a room, or tilt a wedge
Of mountainside, and flip it upside-down . . .

Meths, white spirit, petrol, polish – smells
That led you upward like a spiral stair
Leaving you dizzy in the vaporised
Ice-bright striations of a sky, the glare
Of shattered sunlight on the pitching swells

Of a distant sea, its yellow shoreline
Darkened by gliding shadow clouds, or by
The sliding bridal trains of draining waves –
Somewhere a disturbance, a harsh human cry,
And one man less climbs out than waded in.

ON THE ROAD TO
CHENONCEAUX

A grey Mercedes comes and vanishes,
Its hum declines along the empty road
Where melting pitch gleams through the surface dust.
Wind plays the light on rustling leaves – grey, green,
And a blue that isn't there, but seems to be.

Another colour flickers in the hedge,
Obscure behind embroideries of buds
And a scent that's lost as soon as it's discovered;
Elusive, but defined by its apparel,
Event that may have never taken place –

Beside the hedge, an unattended pile
Of watermelons catches and keeps the light
Among the dappled shadows of its orbs –
One is so huge, its rind has split apart
And through the gash pink darkens into scarlet

As if to show how sensuous is the core
Of all veiled things: look at the hedge again,
Find what eludes deficiency of sense,
Depict the known and not the imagined
Or the desired, and in a language of plain fact –

Radicle, plumule, and cotyledon
Cased in the integument of seed,
And the slow absorption of the mineral earth;
Carpel, stamen, petal, sepal and leaf,
Keys to unlock the doors of a given world –

Another car comes by and disappears,
Before it's gone, it shimmers in the haze
Of heat that rises from the empty road;
The wind still plays the light from grey to green
Through a blue that isn't there, but seems to be.

CELLO MUSIC

You're visiting a castle. There's a lake,
A hill, a wood, gardens, a herd of deer,
And then inside, paintings of lakes and hills,
Mounted antlers, the cornucopian year
Carved in four oak festoons – you're here to slake

A once-yearly thirst for the concentrate
Of irretrievable times. It doesn't work –
Like drinking to get drunk and staying sober;
The trees don't make a wood, that rain-pocked murk
Won't turn into a lake, you can't translate

These stones into a castle . . . Time to go;
The windows darken as you set off home –
Room after room, the blaze of chandeliers
Sliding away like honey from a comb,
Days out of a life, or any slow

Extinguishing of fire . . . Much later on,
Reaching a village with a puddled street
And wet bronze soldier, slowing down, you see
Framed in a window misted by the heat
Of a single lamp and her own action,

A woman playing the cello, all alone
In a plain room at a plain brass music stand,
But cradling rose-grained curves and scrolls of wood
Like something alive; one splayed-out, powerful hand
Trembling where her blood pulses into the tone

As she plunges and draws back the bow –
She seems incongruous in this dead place,
Its only light her own. You cannot hear
But you can see the music in her face,
Its ecstasies – you see it now

And it's not a face you see, but a lake
Mottled like jade with lily-pads, dead leaves,
Gold in a silk-tailed swish scrolled through the black —
You climb a hill, and underfoot thick sheaves
Of wet grass furrow silver like the track

A finger leaves in velvet. Browsing deer
Move like a forest carpet come to life —
Split chestnut eyes, bare branches, wet red leaves
Dotted with melting snow, you catch a whiff
Of wild rose, then white battlements appear.

THE BURNT ONES

We lay on the dark lawn watching
Green go luminous then grey,
Dusk-hush, sharp moon, night-scented flowers
Ushered out the last day –

If I knew then what I know now
I'd have stayed there forever,
There between the cobbled walls
And the flint-grey river –

Too much of summer
Leaves us and everything dead;
Bleaches the earth, dismantles
Each crisp hydrangea head –

Night's fricatives, the creak of beams,
Glass rattled, would nothing halt?
A daddy-long-legs skittered
Down my back like sprinkled salt

Daybreak was red and restless,
Mid-morning grey,
We cleaned up in silence,
Packed, and drove away.

PICTURE OF A GIRL

I lie on the dirty white candlewick
You so disliked, thinking of you at your best;
Among animals mostly – Absalom
Whose high, unearthly screech you mimicked once
So fluently, he swooped from his chimney perch
To strut before us on the rain-fresh lawn,
Rustling green plumage as if a mate
Had bloomed there like the cêpes and chanterelles . . .
And then the cats; Babette, whose dynasty
Had frayed the Morris hangings into shreds –
I remember you struggling to hold all twelve
Still in your lap for a photograph;
That night you giggled quietly in your sleep –
Lovely transparent dreamer, I could see
The singed-beige kittens tumbling there again . . .

Now I recede, the years are like rough stones
Glazed to a moonstone glimmer by the sea,
Fantastical – Absalom cries again,
I hear that garden crackling in the rain,
Pale dusty green mimosa's saffron burrs
Turning to paste as they brush our clothes,
Quicksilver raindrops on the soft peach fuzz –
We lived well, I remember starched linen,
Silver, the flayed blue hearts of hot-house figs,
My profligate goddess stooping where a marrow
Had burst with rain, and spilt its sequin seeds,
The clouds pitted like granite, but tissue-light,
Heaving their slow collisions in the skies,
And where the pond froze up one winter night
Big golden carp alive beneath the ice.

Caught twice at once by that trick of the unborn,
Infatuation, he is first with Jane
In Arkansas. The bearskin on their bed
Turns into a bear again, till dawn.
She is his anodyne – blonde, brown-eyed, sane,
Breeding her golden pheasants in a shed,
Content with that, and the stream-laced hills,
Their milt of yellow diamonds, the Trail of Tears
Her Cherokee forefathers flooded through . . .
They fill a jar with honey till it spills –
That night he hears the trash upturned by bears,
And cries out, wanting London air, and Sue –

– whose life's a nervous fibrillation and
Entanglement of too much reading, thought,
Adrenalin . . . Her room's bright colours clash
Vibrantly, and when he takes her hand
He sometimes feels an armature go taut;
An empty metal fruitbowl streaked with ash
Stands by the bed, a shot-down flight of books
Goes dusty on the floor – they watch forked streams
Of condensation lace a grimy pane;
He needs her so – his life is like blue sparks
Crackling between two poles; that night he dreams
Of yellow diamonds, Arkansas, and Jane.

BRIDAL

You've felt this before – eyes wide open
   In a strange bedroom, pitch-black,
A moment's panic till the soul slides back
   Into the body, or again
Mid-sentence as you gather in the slack
Of a circuitous argument, to crush
   An enemy, when suddenly you find
That brilliant *coup de grâce* has slipped your mind,
   Leaving you stranded, a cruel hush
Descending, as you feel the seconds grind

   Down to a halt . . . So it is you stand
     Jarred out of memory, beside
This veiled apotheosis of a bride,
    Your hand held up beside her hand,
Lily-of-the-Valley bunched above the wide
Cream wake of tulle that ripples through a sea
   Of faces so similar they clash
Like adjacent notes – faces in lavish
   Frames of burnished fur and millinery,
Metallic faces, vulcanised in cash –

   Money, breeding, the lace-covered prize
     Rustling like a big white rose;
Prime of England – and what if, blind, you chose
    What others crave with open eyes –
Stoles, medals, diamonds – how can you refuse?
Golden, laburnum-fringed, the organ pipes
   Drown hesitation in a great swell
Of sound that sends a tremor through her veil;
   How can you wait to taste those lips,
Taste acquiescence on your tongue? 'I will,

I do' – words in a confetti swirl
    Dissolve the present, and thrust
You forward into daylight while the dust
    Of a life left starts to settle:
You stand and blink, a man without a past –
Choice was illusion too; look how the father
    Looms up from a dazzling winter sun –
Grin of a species welcoming its own;
    One hand on your shoulder, in the other
A champagne bottle smoking like a gun.